1

PRIVACY AND CIVIL LIBERTIES OVERSIGHT BOARD

PUBLIC MEETING

I0410893

Report on the Telephone Records Program

Conducted under Section 215

Of the USA PATRIOT Act

And on the Operations of the

Foreign Intelligence Surveillance Court

January 23, 2014

The public meeting was held at George Washington

University, Marvin Center, Room 309, 800 21st,

Street, NW, Washington, D.C. 20052 commencing

at 1:00 p.m.

Reported by: Lynne Livingston

2

1   BOARD MEMBERS

2

3   David Medine, Chairman

4   Rachel Brand

5   Patricia Wald

6   James Dempsey

7   Elisebeth Collins Cook

8

9

10

11

12

13

14

15

16

17

18

19

20

21

22

1   PROCEEDINGS

2   MR. MEDINE: Good afternoon. Welcome to

3   an open meeting of the Privacy and Civil Liberties

4   Oversight Board. It's 1:00 p.m., and the date is

5   January 23rd, 2014.

6   We're at the George Washington University

7   Marvin Center, room 309, located at 800 21st

8   Street, N.W., Washington, D.C.

9   (Interruption in the proceedings)

10   MR. MEDINE: The meeting was announced in

11   a Federal Register notice on January 16th, 2014.

12   As Chairman, I will be the presiding

13   officer.

14   All five Board members are present and

15   there is a quorum. The Board members are Rachel

16   Brand, Elisebeth Cook, James Dempsey and Patricia

17   Wald.

18   I will now call the hearing to order.

19   All in favor of opening the Report say aye.

20   (Aye)

21   MR. MEDINE: Upon receiving unanimous

22   consent to proceed, we will now proceed. The

4

1   Board has convened today to formally adopt its

2   Report on the telephone records program conducted

3   under Section 215 of the USA PATRIOT Act, and on

4   the operations of the Foreign Intelligence

5   Surveillance Court.

6   Now before starting our discussion of the

7   Report, the Board has conducted a many months

8   study of two NSA programs and had an opportunity

9   to interact extensively with the intelligence

10   community.

11   I want to emphasize that we have found

12   nothing but a dedicated group of men and women

13   working in the intelligence community who are

14   dedicated to protecting the country and protecting

15   our civil rights.

16   We have not found evidence of misconduct

17   during the course of our investigation. We have

18   comments about the programs as they operate, but

19   we believe the individuals who operate the

20   programs have operated in good faith.

21   We have also received extensive

22   cooperation from the executive branch in providing

1   access to the classified materials we've

2   requested, and briefings as appropriate.

3   As background, in response to

4   congressional and presidential requests in June of

5   this year, the Privacy and Civil Liberties

6   Oversight Board undertook an in-depth study of

7   Section 215 and Section 702 programs, as well as

8   the operations of the FISA court.

9   The report on Section 702, which will be

10   unclassified, will follow in the next several

11   months.

12   This study of the two programs and the

13   FISA court included briefings with officials from

14   the Office of the Director for National

15   Intelligence, the NSA, the Department of Justice,

16   the Federal Bureau of Investigations, and the

17   Central Intelligence Agency.

18   Board members also met with White House

19   staff, a former presiding judge of the FISC,

20   academics, privacy and civil liberties advocates,

21   technology and communication companies, and trade

22   associations.

6

1   The Board has been provided access to

2 classified opinions of the FISC, of various

3 Inspector General reports, and additional

4 classified documents relating to the operation and

5 effectiveness of the programs.

6   As part of its study consistent with its

7 statutory mandate to operate publicly where

8 possible, the Board held two public forums.

9   In order to ensure the accuracy of our

10 report, the Board provided a draft copy of the

11 description of the operations of the Foreign

12 Intelligence Surveillance Court to the court staff

13 to verify the statements that were made.

14   The Board also provided draft analysis of

15 the efficacy of the Section 215 program, but not

16 the conclusions and recommendations, to the

17 intelligence community to ensure that our factual

18 statements were correct and complete.

19   While the Board's Report was subject to

20 classification review, none of the changes

21 resulting from that process affected our analysis

22 or recommendations.

1   As an indication of the Board's

2   independence, there was no outside review of the

3   substance of the Board's analysis and

4   recommendations.

5   Pursuant to the Board's statutory duty to

6   advise the President and elements of the executive

7   branch to ensure that privacy and civil liberties

8   are appropriately considered in the development

9   and implementation of legislation and policies,

10   and to provide advice on proposals to retain or

11   enhance a particular power, the PCLOB and the

12   staff met with White House senior staff to discuss

13   the Board's tentative conclusions on December 5th.

14   On January 8th, the full Board met with

15   the President, Vice President and senior staff to

16   present the Board's conclusions and views of

17   individual members before the President's speech

18   last week.

19   To give you the bottom line of our

20   Report, the majority of the Privacy and Civil

21   Liberties Oversight Board believes that the 215

22   program is inconsistent with the statute that

8

1   authorizes it on a number of grounds.

2   First, the telephone records acquired

3   under the program have no connection to a specific

4   FBI investigation at the time of their collection.

5   Second, because the records are collected

6   in bulk, potentially encompassing all telephone

7   records across the nation, they cannot be regarded

8   as relevant to a particular investigation or to

9   any investigation of the FBI.

10   Third, the program operates by putting

11   telephone companies under an obligation to furnish

12   new calling records, as opposed to the statute's

13   requirement that they only provide existing

14   records and not ongoing production.

15   Fourth, the statute only authorizes the

16   FBI to collect information from the telephone

17   providers, and yet it's the NSA that receives the

18   information.

19   We also looked at the Electronic

20   Communications Privacy Act that restricts

21   telephone providers from providing information to

22   the government except under certain specific

1   exceptions. There is no exception for the 215

2   program.

3   And finally, we considered whether

4   Congress's extension of the deadline for the

5   expiration of the 215 program on two occasions

6   indicated congressional approval of the operation

7   of that program, and a majority of the Board

8   concluded that that was not the case.

9   So again, the majority of the Board takes

10   the view that the 215 program is not authorized by

11   statute, that it raises series constitutional and

12   privacy concerns and has not demonstrated

13   sufficient effectiveness to continue in operation

14   on a permanent basis.

15   Based on legal, constitutional and policy

16   reasons, a majority of the Board recommend that it

17   be discontinued in its current form.

18   Going forward, telephone metadata could

19   be obtained directly from providers under other

20   legal authorities, but the Board does not

21   recommend imposing additional retention

22   requirements on those providers.

1   The Board unanimously recommends some

2   immediate changes be made to the program. First,

3   that records be kept for only three years and not

4   the current five years, that only two hops instead

5   of three hops be permitted in doing record

6   searches, that reasonable, articulable suspicion

7   determinations, the RAS determinations, be

8   provided that justifies the search of records, be

9   provided to the FISC court after the fact for the

10   FISC court to review and determine whether those

11   were appropriate searches, and that the records

12   maintained by the NSA be only subject to searches

13   based on reasonable, articulable suspicion, even

14   if they're in the database of the NSA.

15   On the Foreign Intelligence Surveillance

16   Court we unanimously recommend the creation of a

17   Special Advocate drawn from a panel of private

18   attorneys who appear when invited by the FISC

19   judges in cases involving novel and significant

20   applications or other matters where the judge

21   would find such additional views helpful.

22   We also want to recommend expanding the

1   opportunities for appellate review of FISC

2   decisions to the Foreign Intelligence Surveillance

3   Court of Review, as well as to the Supreme Court.

4   We've also focused on transparency of

5   government in the operations of these programs,

6   and going forward we recommend declassification of

7   FISC decisions on an ongoing basis so the public

8   benefits from the court's reasoning in approving

9   particular programs.

10   And we also recommend going back and

11   declassifying significant FISC decisions, but

12   recognizing that involves significant resources,

13   and have that kept in mind in terms of the process

14   and the time frame for declassifying those

15   decisions.

16   We also, a majority of the Board also

17   believes that the scope of legal surveillance

18   authorities affecting Americans should be made

19   public and determined from the face of the

20   statutes.

21   I'm going to go through the twelve

22   specific recommendations that the Board makes in

1   its report.

2   The first, again, is the government

3   should end its 215 bulk telephone records program.

4   Second, the government should immediately

5   implement additional privacy safeguards in

6   operating the 215 bulk program.

7   Third, Congress should enact legislation

8   enabling the court, Foreign Intelligence

9   Surveillance Court to hear independent views.

10   Fourth, Congress should enact legislation

11   to expand opportunities for appellate review of

12   those court's decisions.

13   Fifth, the court should take full

14   advantage of existing authorities to obtain

15   technical assistance and expand opportunities for

16   legal input from outside parties.

17   Sixth, to the maximum extent possible

18   consistent with national security, the government

19   should release new decisions, and as I mentioned

20   before, declassify prior decisions of the court.

21   And I'm sorry, that's also seventh.

22   Eight, the Attorney General should

1   regularly and publicly report information

2   regarding the operation of the Special Advocate

3   program to ensure that it's being used

4   effectively.

5   Ninth, the government should work with

6   Internet service providers and other companies

7   that regularly receive FISC, FISA production

8   orders to develop rules permitting those companies

9   to voluntarily disclose certain statistical

10   information about the government's requests,

11   keeping in mind the need to protect national

12   security.

13   Ten, the Attorney General should inform

14   the Privacy and Civil Liberties Oversight Board of

15   the government's activities under FISA.

16   Eleven, the Board urges the government to

17   begin developing principles and criteria for

18   transparency.

19   And twelve, the scope of surveillance

20   authorities affecting Americans should be made

21   public.

22   At this point I'll give individual Board

1   members an opportunity to express their views.

2   Mr. Dempsey.

3   MR. DEMPSEY: Thank you, Mr. Chairman.

4   And I want to express my appreciation to all the

5   other members of the Board. We've worked

6   remarkably hard with a tiny staff over the course

7   of the past six or seven months since these

8   programs were brought to public attention.

9   And we've received, as the Chairman said,

10   throughout the process we've received the full

11   cooperation of the executive branch and of the

12   intelligence agencies. And I would say we've met

13   many, many fine people who are working every day

14   to keep us all safe, and nothing in our report is

15   intended in any way as a criticism of them.

16   In fact, we offer our report in the

17   spirit that we found from these public servants,

18   which was their desire to live within the law

19   while protecting the national security. And

20   that's our goal here as well.

21   When I first heard last June about the

22   fact that the FISA court had authorized bulk

1   collection of information about all domestic and

2   international phone calls of essentially all

3   Americans my initial reaction was, well, the

4   court's authorized it so it must be legal. And

5   it's logical to assume that it would be effective

6   if we have all this data, the bad guys clearly use

7   telephones to communicate with each other, and

8   it's only logical that we can find the unknowns

9   and find otherwise undetectable connections that

10 would help disrupt plots and provide critical

11 information to the counterterrorism mission.

12   After months of studying the program

13 however, and after our staff conducted what is the

14 most exhaustive analysis yet done of the statutory

15 basis for the program, and the most in-depth

16 analysis ever done that we're aware of, of the

17 results of the program, I found, and the majority

18 of the Board has concluded that there are really

19 two immovable objects, two things that you just

20 can't get around.

21   One, the statute that's cited for the

22 program does not support it.

1   And secondly, the results of the program

2   have been limited, falling far short of the highly

3   desirable outcome promised for it.

4   Faced with the overwhelming disconnect

5   between the statute and the program as conducted

6   and given the limited results, we concluded that

7   the program should be ended, allowing for a

8   transition period, as the President has called

9   for.

10   Now we spent a lot of time looking at the

11 statutory analysis. Thirty-eight judges over the

12 past seven years -- I'm sorry, 37 times over the

13 past seven years, 17 federal judges have examined

14 this issue and found the program to be legal, but

15 until the Snowden leaks not one of them had

16 written an opinion explaining how the program fit

17 into the statute.

18   And still to this day no judge has

19 addressed all of the problems we identified in our

20 statutory analysis.

21   At this point proponents and opponents of

22 the program have the same problem, the program has

17

1   been shoe-horned into a statute not designed for

2   it.

3   And now, given the President's

4   announcement last week, we, the Congress, the

5   executive branch, the court are looking for a new

6   program, with a lot of room for debate about what

7   it should look like.

8   I do not think we should just accept bulk

9   collection as a given and layer on additional

10   protections. We have to go back to the

11   fundamental question, should we be collecting bulk

12   data and under what legal standards.

13   Now despite the highest respect that I

14   have for the decent people working under pressure

15   who brought this program under the statute and who

16   have shaped it over the past twelve years, or the

17   past seven years, I think the policy process was

18   flawed.

19   The process took the word relevant and

20   expanded it into a new meaning that it never had

21   before. It took the concept of a subpoena, which

22   was intended as a limiting concept, and gave it a

1   meaning that it has never had before.

2   And then faced with the question of

3   effectiveness we've said, or defenders of the

4   program have said that it can be justified because

5   its negative results provide a peace of mind, or

6   because it reaffirms what we already know, or it

7   might work someday.

8   As a matter of policy the concept of

9   relevance is not the right basis for big data

10   collection. The analogy of a grand jury subpoena,

11   which I believe was meant to limit the scope of

12   this authority, is not the right analogy for an

13   ongoing collection program.

14   The standard of peace of mind is not the

15   right standard for assessing the effectiveness of

16   a program like this.

17   And finally, the process that Congress

18   went through here, again, absolutely with the best

19   of intentions and working very hard to keep us all

20   safe, the process was flawed.

21   There was a private understanding of what

22   the program was and how it would work and what its

1   elements were that was not at all reflected in the

2   public record.

3   In fact, the public record would have led

4   you to believe that Section 215 meant something

5   quite different. And the plain words of the

6   statute would lead you to believe that it was

7   about something different.

8   So in my view we have to dig ourselves

9   out of that hole. We have to have the debate, and

10   the President has called for the debate about

11   whether we should have, in my opinion, bulk

12   collection and then what the standard should be

13   for it.

14   I'll say one thing, two ideas have

15   emerged, which is the idea that the program would

16   be okay if the data were held by another entity,

17   either by the telephone companies themselves or by

18   some third party that would be created.

19   And certainly if the idea would be that

20   the phone companies would be required to hold

21   data, or if a third party were created to hold the

22   data, I see no privacy benefit to that at all.

1   And I think it's important to recognize that at

2   the get-go, that there's no easy out on this

3   program.

4   Saying let somebody else other than the

5   government hold it does not answer any of the

6   questions that need to be answered, how much, how

7   long, who gets it, under what standard, how do you

8   protect the security of it, how do you enforce it,

9   who oversees compliance, what liability measures

10   apply, etcetera.

11   So I'm pleased that we're here today. We

12   all have to recognize that this is one way station

13   in a long journey. The President has said that he

14   wanted to resolve this by the end of March when

15   the current orders expire. I don't think there's

16   any way that we can have the debate that's

17   necessary and resolve these questions by the end

18   of March, but as a member of this Board I look

19   forward to participating in that debate as it

20   occurs.

21   MR. MEDINE: Thank you. Judge Wald.

22   MS. WALD: Let me just pick up a few end

1   pieces here about what I think are the important

2   things in the report in case all of you don't get

3   to read all 237 pages of it.

4   First, on the legality, which I think is

5   probably one of the, I know is one of the most

6   controversial aspects of our Report. We have two

7   dissenters on our Board on that subject. The

8   question has even been raised, why do we get into

9   the legality and why didn't we just stick to the

10   policy.

11   And I think the answer to that is an

12   important one to think about, and that's that our

13   mandate in our statute is to look at whether or

14   not the programs are and are implemented in a way

15   to be consistent with law.

16   And I think that a real civil liberties

17   question arises if a law, no matter how fairly it

18   is implemented, turns out not to have been

19   authorized at all to begin with.

20   And for all the reasons which I won't go

21   into, I agree with the majority analysis that the

22   wording in 215, paraphrasing some words the

1   Supreme Court has used in other cases where it

2   says an agency has over-read the statute and was

3   not authorized to do something under the statute

4   that it did.

5   The words like relevant simply don't bear

6   the weight of what's been put upon them. When you

7   add that to the fact that there was no public

8   discussion whatsoever, you could read the

9   legislative history until you're blue in the face

10   and you wouldn't have any idea that this was a

11   program that was going to be authorized by it.

12   So I think it was very important that we

13   do discuss the legality. I believe we discussed

14   it in more detail than any other authority that I

15   know about. And obviously some people may not be

16   convinced, but we certainly were.

17   Now the reason we have a

18   constitutionality section in there, I think even

19   though we don't come out with a result saying it

20   is constitutional or it is not constitutional, we

21   say that the authorities, certainly under existing

22   law had the right to proceed on the basis that

1   there was precedent in the law to undergird the

2   program.

3   On the other hand, I think it was

4   important for the fact that Congress is going to

5   be considering an overhaul of the law that the

6   constitutional arguments, the trends be at least

7   elaborated on, and I think we did do that.

8   The fact of whether or not you can depend

9   upon Smith v. Maryland and the Miller cases, which

10   go back twenty or more years, twenty, twenty-five

11   years, in light of not new precedent exactly on

12   the point, but cases like Jones, which dealt with

13   the global location instruments, that actually at

14   least many members, some members of the Supreme

15   Court are concerned about the fact that you might

16   without warrants be able to track indefinitely all

17   the movements, in that case it was the movements.

18   But the telephone numbers could, in the

19   opinion of many experts that we heard in our

20   various public forums, also be the basis for the

21   same kind of information.

22   So that I think the constitutional law

1   discussion, while we didn't come out with a

2   recommendation we're saying this is an

3   unconstitutional program, which one judge has

4   already said, but we did not follow that, I think,

5   I hope is a contribution to the congressional

6   legislation that will come up.

7   I don't think the law is going to stand

8   still on those old cases, which really dealt with

9   individual situations and not with taking the

10 telephone numbers over a period of five years of

11 everybody in the United States.

12   When we got to the policy discussion,

13 which at least I think everybody agrees was the

14 reason we were set up, no dissents on that, I

15 think the thing that I would emphasize was that,

16 although as Chairman Medine pointed out, we

17 certainly found no evidence of any kind of

18 intentional misuse of the program.

19   Some inadvertent uses were found by the

20 FISC court itself in released decisions, but

21 nothing suggesting that people were looking to

22 privately exploit or to politically intimidate

1   anybody with this information.

2   Nonetheless, I think our discussion about

3   the potential danger emphasizes what I think is

4   the big question underlying 215, which is going to

5   come up again and again and again, and that is the

6   differentiation between collection and use.

7   Because the collection of the information, which

8   many of our experts suggested the collection

9   itself changes things, even if it's the fact that

10   the government has this mass of information even

11   if it doesn't use it in any way detrimental to

12   anybody, it changes the power structure.

13   It has the potential down the road, I

14   mean these people are wonderful and honest and

15   stuff, but I'm probably the oldest person in the

16   room and I could go back a couple of decades, and

17   it is possible when administrations change,

18   etcetera, to have, if you've got that big -- it's

19   like build a field and they will come kind of

20   thing, as to it's there for the use.

21   Now what I think the reply to all of that

22   is that there are all kinds of controls on the

1   use, and there are some controls on the use, and

2   there's some good controls on the use. We might

3   tinker with them and change some of them, but

4   basically there is a control for the use.

5   But I think this basic notion as the

6   government seeks to, when it does, collect more

7   and more databanks on the citizens, the whole

8   basic question, which 215 raises, of the

9   collection itself versus the misuse. So I think

10   that's there.

11   I won't say -- two other points I'll

12   mention, only very briefly. One, I think we did

13   come to a consensus on the FISC court and I think

14   it's a good one. It's not as extreme as some of

15   the proposals for putting a whole new institution

16   akin to the public defenders in there. We thought

17   that because the FISC court actually handles,

18   handles very well and without anybody raising any

19   controversy about it, hundreds, whatever it is, of

20   individual, individual applications for warrants

21   based upon some kind of particularized statutory

22   criteria, they only have, we were told by one of

1   the judges, one of the former judges, about ten or

2   twelve cases that raise the kind of questions that

3   are in 215.

4   So we thought having a core of expert

5   private attorneys who could be called in. And we

6   also found, perceived we found a willingness on

7   the part of the FISC judges, if that were ready

8   there, to call upon them when they needed it.

9   Remember, the statistic was raised by Jim

10   about however many opinions, however many judges,

11   I've forgotten now, but none of those judges had

12   the benefit of an adversary. The only two cases

13   in which we've had 215 looked at have been the

14   district court judges who came to opposite

15   conclusions, in which case there were adversaries.

16   So I think the notion of having an

17   adversary available, and it's one we could all

18   agree upon, including mechanisms for appeal.

19   There have only been in the history of the FISC

20   court in, what is it, thirty years now, more than

21   thirty years, there have only been two appeals to

22   review court. So I think we wanted to expedite

1   those.

2   Finally, my last point is actually I

3   think one of the more important things. It's one

4   I'm sorry to say we're not completely in agreement

5   on, is the transparency section. We have some

6   parts of it I think we all agree, greater

7   transparency for FISC.

8   But I do think it's very important for

9   the future that there be a culture of making, when

10   a law is passed that is going to be used, or when

11   its use comes about after the law has passed, that

12   is going to affect a huge group of Americans about

13   whom there's no suspicion at all, not even an

14   affiliation with anybody or any contact with

15   anybody, but it's going to blanket it and provide

16   information, which while it may not be as explicit

17   as content still does have some informative value,

18   that the framework of that law and its purpose,

19   without the operational details, be made a matter

20   of record in the public debate.

21   Obviously people are worried about

22   national security and they don't want operational

1   details, but I think we have to watch out that we

2   don't let a kind of secret law regime creep into

3   our jurisprudence, except for a few instances

4   where it may be absolutely, absolutely necessary.

5   MR. MEDINE: Beth Cook.

6   MS. COLLINS COOK: Thank you. I also

7   commend the work of my colleagues and our plucky

8   staff. And I've assured them that the phrase

9   plucky is the highest compliment that I can give.

10   I also appreciate the opportunity to

11   express my own views and I have also set forth

12   these views in a short separate statement

13   accompanying the majority's Report.

14   As previously indicated, I agree with ten

15   of the twelve recommendations of the Report.

16   First, I agree with the careful recommendations we

17   have made with respect to the FISA court, as well

18   as additional transparency about our legal

19   framework. I believe both of these will increase

20   public confidence in our national security

21   efforts.

22   I hope we can work with the agencies and

1   with Congress going forward to implement these

2   unanimous recommendations in a responsible way.

3   Specifically, I join the recommendation

4   for a Special Advocate because participation of

5   that advocate in a given case or a given appeal is

6   left to the discretion of the court, and because

7   we have recognized that our recommendations must,

8   quote, take into account the imperative of secrecy

9   in the application of some of the nation's most

10 sensitive intelligence collection techniques, the

11 importance of speed in responding to often

12 fast-breaking events posing severe risk to the

13 national security, the resource limits faced by

14 the court and its judges, and constitutional

15 issues.

16   Similarly, I join the transparency

17 recommendations, except recommendation 12, only

18 because of our caution that they should be

19 implemented to the, quote, extent possible

20 consistent with national security.

21   Second, given the potential risks to

22 privacy of bulk data collection on this scale

1   weighed against the potential benefits of the

2   program, I agree with the majority's

3   recommendations to modify the operations of the

4   Section 215 program.

5   I view the development of this modified

6   program as an ideal opportunity for the Board to

7   fulfill its statutory advisory role.

8   More broadly, bulk collection of data on

9   this scale raises serious questions, but given the

10   increasing threats we see, including in the cyber

11   arena, we are only at the beginning of a

12   discussion of how best to answer those questions.

13   As I noted however, I do not join the

14   majority's legal analysis, either statutory or

15   constitutional, its discussion of the efficacy of

16   the program, or its recommendation to shut down

17   the Section 215 program.

18   First, I believe that the program rests

19   on a permissible interpretation of the statute and

20   so far as I am aware every federal judge to have

21   considered the question has reached the same

22   conclusion.

1   And I would add as an example as to one

2   point that is of concern to the majority, the

3   relevance analysis. That analysis has always been

4   a contextual analysis, and the statute tells you

5   to look at the investigations as the cornerstone

6   for the relevance analysis.

7   Here these authorized investigations that

8   are the statutory touchstone for the statutory

9   analysis are unlike any investigations we have

10 ever seen. So it stands to reason that the

11 interpretation of relevance could likewise be

12 unlike what we have previously seen.

13   By the same token, I consider much of the

14 Board's constitutional analysis to be speculative

15 and unnecessary, focused on potential changes to

16 Fourth Amendment jurisprudence or the First

17 Amendment implications of programs that do not

18 exist.

19   I think the program itself represented a

20 good faith effort to subject a potentially

21 controversial program to both judicial and

22 legislative oversight and should be commended.

1   The program was authorized by federal judges and

2   subject to meaningful executive, judicial and

3   congressional oversight.

4   Although the NSA made mistakes, the court

5   and Congress were notified, corrective action was

6   taken and the program repeatedly reauthorized.

7   I also take a different view from the

8   majority as to the efficacy and utility of the

9   Section 215 program. In today's world of never-

10   ending and varied threats, I believe a tool such

11   as Section 215 that allows investigators to triage

12   and focus on those who are more likely to be doing

13   harm to or in the United States, or allows

14   investigators to dismiss potential homeland

15   connections to ongoing terror threats or plots is

16   valuable.

17   And as the majority has also indicated,

18   Section 215 has been used in conjunction with

19   other authorities to identify additional leads and

20   supply confirming or supplemental information

21   about our adversaries, which makes it a valuable

22   program.

1   In other words, Section 215 has and will

2   allow us to connect the dots and paint a fuller

3   picture of our adversaries.

4   As I noted in my separate statement

5   however, I would urge the government to think very

6   seriously about how to evaluate and explain the

7   relative value of its various counterterrorism

8   authorities and programs.

9   So where do we go from here? Although

10 the program does involve vast amounts of data,

11 that data does not include the content of

12 communications, nor does it include the identity

13 of the individuals associated with the call

14 records collected.

15   Let me repeat that. The identities of

16 the individuals are not associated with the call

17 records when those call records are sent to the

18 NSA. So no content, no identities.

19   Given those facts and my own

20 understanding of the statute, I do not believe

21 that the program poses the same types of risk to

22 privacy as does the majority and would not shut

1   down the program for either legal or policy

2   reasons.

3   However, as I noted before, bulk

4   collection does raise privacy concerns and it is

5   based on these concerns that I have joined the

6   unanimous recommendations to modify the operation

7   of the program.

8   I would also support an alternative that

9   poses fewer risks to privacy, but I echo my

10   colleague's words here, that this is not a simple

11   question nor a simple answer.

12   In that regard I too would sound a note

13   of caution about alternatives that have been

14   mentioned to date.

15   I would have concerns about counting on

16   the providers to hold the records as an adequate

17   substitute. The same amount of information would

18   likely not be available and less and less will

19   likely be available over time. Companies do not

20   want this and I am hard pressed to see how this

21   would help with their customers' concerns.

22   I think the end result will be

36

1   significant pressure to impose a data retention

2   requirement which potentially poses more threats

3   to privacy.

4   Similarly, keeping the records at a third

5   party would also raise serious concerns.

6   Providing sufficient security for the information

7   would necessitate a framework that would be the

8   functional equivalent of the government holding

9   the data. Thank you.

10   MR. MEDINE: Rachel Brand.

11   MS. BRAND: Thank you, Mr. Chairman. I'd

12   like to start by commending the rest of the Board

13   and our tiny staff for getting this Report out

14   while we still work to set up our brand new

15   federal agency. It has not been an easy task.

16   I have published a short separate

17   statement of my views, which is included in the

18   Board's Report, which is available to you in the

19   back of the room. I'll try to be brief in

20   summarizing those views here.

21   I concur in almost all of the Board's

22   recommendations, and I am pleased that so many of

1   them were unanimous.

2   Most importantly, I join the Board's

3   recommendations for immediately modifying the

4   Section 215 program because I believe those

5   changes will reduce privacy concerns without

6   sacrificing the operational value of the program.

7   However, I dissent from two of the

8   Report's recommendations, including its

9   recommendation to shut down the Section 215

10   program without establishing an adequate

11   alternative.

12   My dissent results in part from two

13   overarching concerns. First, I'm concerned the

14   Report gives insufficient weight to the need for a

15   proactive approach to combating terrorism.

16   Second, I hope the Report will not

17   contribute to the wild swings of the pendulum that

18   occur too often in policy-making on national

19   security issues.

20   After a terrorist attack the public

21   points fingers at the government for failing to

22   prevent it. As memory fades or after an

1   unauthorized leak of classified information, the

2   public demands that the government pull back its

3   counterterrorism efforts.

4   The pendulum seems to be going back in

5   that direction now, but I have no doubt that if

6   there is another large scale terrorist attack on

7   the United States the public will demand to know

8   why the government did not prevent it. This

9   dynamic is nothing new, but it's an unfortunate

10   way to craft national security policy.

11   Turning to my reasons for dissenting from

12   the Board's recommendation to shut down the

13   Section 215 program.

14   First, I do not agree with the Board that

15   the program is not statutorily authorized. The

16   question of whether the language of Section 215

17   authorizes the metadata program is a difficult

18   one, I will grant that.

19   But the government's interpretation of

20   the statute is reasonable and was made in good

21   faith by numerous officials in two administrations

22   of different parties, who take seriously their

1   responsibility to protect the American people from

2   terrorism.

3   In any event, it's been upheld by every

4   single federal judge to have considered the

5   statutory question, both in the FISA court and in

6   regular U.S. district court.

7   As an institutional matter I do not

8   believe this is a question on which this Board can

9   meaningfully contribute. This legal question will

10   be resolved in the courts, not by us. We are much

11   better equipped to assess whether the program is

12   sound as a policy matter.

13   Turning to the program's

14   constitutionality, I agree with the Board's

15   ultimate conclusion that the program is

16   constitutional under governing Supreme Court case

17   law. I don't see the need to join on to its

18   analysis in light of that.

19   Of course the government must seriously

20   consider whether it should operate this program,

21   even if it can do so.

22   Whether the program is good policy is a

1   question squarely within this Board's core

2   mandate, but I do not agree with the Board's

3   conclusion on that question either. Whether it

4   should continue boils down to whether its

5   potential intrusion on privacy interests is

6   outweighed by the national security value of the

7   program.

8   Starting with the privacy question, on

9   the one hand, any collection program on this scale

10   gives me pause. Metadata can be revealing.

11   Whenever the government possesses this much

12   information it could theoretically be used for

13   dangerous purposes in the wrong hands without

14   adequate oversight.

15   And even if there is no actual privacy

16   violation if information is collected but never

17   viewed, as is true of the vast majority of the

18   information collected by this program, collecting

19   this much data creates at least a risk of a

20   serious privacy intrusion.

21   This is why I joined the Board's

22   recommendation for immediately modifying the

1   program if it continues.

2   On the other hand, the government has not

3   collected content of any communication under this

4   program. It does not collect any personally

5   identifying information at all. What seems to

6   have gotten lost in the debate is what Beth

7   mentioned early, which is that this program is

8   literally a system of numbers with no names

9   associated with any of them.

10   In addition, the program operates within

11   remarkably strict safeguards and limitations

12   already. The Board's report and my separate

13   statement discuss them and I won't repeat them

14   here. But with those safeguards already in place

15   and with the additional safeguards the Board

16   recommends, I think the actual intrusion on

17   privacy interests will be quite small.

18   On the other side of the equation is the

19   national security value of the program. I don't

20   agree that there's little, if any, value to the

21   program. There is no easy way to calculate the

22   value of this program. There is no clear test,

1   but the test cannot be whether it has already been

2   the key factor in thwarting a previously unknown

3   terrorist attack. Assessing the benefit of a

4   preventive program like this one requires a

5   longer-term view.

6   Most of this data is never used at all

7   but its immediate availability if it is needed is

8   the program's primary benefit. Its usefulness may

9   not be fully realized until we face another a

10   large-scale terrorist plot. But if that happens,

11   analysts' ability to very quickly scan records

12   from multiple service providers at the same time

13   to establish connections or avoid wasting precious

14   time on futile leads could be critical in

15   thwarting the plot.

16   Considering the evidence of the data from

17   this program could be the key to preventing the

18   next terrorist attack. I cannot recommend

19   shutting it down without an adequate alternative

20   already in place, especially in light of what I

21   view to be the relatively small actual intrusion

22   on privacy interests.

1   That said, if an adequate alternative

2 that reduces privacy concerns can be identified,

3 by all means the government should adopt it.

4   The administration is working on a plan

5 to transfer custody of the data to a third party.

6 I doubt I could support that particular approach.

7 In my view it would make sense only if it both

8 served as an effective alternative and assuaged

9 privacy concerns, and I'm skeptical it could do

10 either.

11   I don't think it could be an effective

12 alternative without requiring the telephone

13 companies to hold the data longer than they

14 otherwise would, but that would create new privacy

15 concerns if the data then became available for a

16 large number of purposes other than national

17 security and would raise a host of other difficult

18 questions.

19   So in my opinion it would be wiser to

20 leave the program as it is with the NSA than to

21 transfer it to the telephone service providers.

22 Thank you.

1   MR. MEDINE: Thank you. Based upon the

2   Board's review of the telephone records program

3   under Section 215 and the operation of the Foreign

4   Intelligence Surveillance Court, we'll now move

5   toward adoption of the Board's recommendations and

6   Report. All in favor of adopting Report

7   recommendations 2 through 11, please say aye.

8   (Aye)

9   MR. MEDINE: Unanimous. All in favor of

10 adopting the Report recommendations 1 and 12,

11 please say aye.

12   (Aye)

13   MR. MEDINE: Opposed?

14   (Nay)

15   MR. MEDINE: Three to two.

16   All in favor of issuing the full Report

17 with additional Board members' statements, please

18 say aye.

19   (Aye)

20   MR. MEDINE: Unanimous. Upon receiving

21 unanimous consent to issue the full Report with

22 the additional Board statements, the Report is now

1   final and will be available on pclob.gov, our

2   website.

3   The Board's activities for the day are

4   now complete. After we adjourn, individual

5   members will be available to meet with members of

6   the press who wish to talk to them.

7   The Board again encourages all interested

8   parties to review our Report online at pclob.gov.

9   A transcript of today's proceedings will also be

10 posted at pclob.gov.

11   I will now call the meeting to adjourn.

12 All in favor of adjourning say aye.

13   (Aye)

14   MR. MEDINE: Upon unanimous consent to

15 adjourn, we are now adjourned. The time is 1:45.

16   (Off the record)

17   Question and Answer Session

18   AUDIENCE MEMBER: Seventeen judges came

19 to 38 opinions or decisions, whatever phrase you

20 used. Why did they come to uphold (inaudible)?

21 Did they not see something that you're seeing?

22   MR. DEMPSEY: Well, 37 of the times were

1 FISA court judges issuing the repeated renewal

2 orders for the programs. So I think if you take

3 38 and divide it by 4, you'll get 6 or 7 years.

4 So that's the length of the program.

5   So it's been repeatedly renewed by the

6 judges, and that's often cited as saying, well, 17

7 judges of the FISA court have looked at it 38

8 times and have approved it.

9   Until after the Snowden leaks not one of

10 those judges had written an opinion, not one of

11 those judges had laid out a legal analysis of the

12 statute.

13   AUDIENCE MEMBER: So you think they did

14 it illegally, is that what you're suggesting?

15   MR. DEMPSEY: No, the judges acted

16 properly. They issued orders which they believed

17 they were authorized to do.

18   What we're saying is their legal analysis

19 was incomplete, at best. And even after the

20 leaks, even after the program became public, the

21 judges who have addressed the statute did not

22 address all of the problems that we have

1   identified, did not address all of the disconnects

2   between the statute and the program.

3   That's why we conclude, with all respect

4   to those judges and with all respect to the

5   government lawyers who presented the arguments to

6   them, we conclude that this statute does not

7   provide an adequate foundation for the program.

8   MR. MEDINE: I just want to add to that

9   in none of those FISA cases was there an adversary

10   to the government in the form of the Special

11   Advocate that we're recommending, someone who

12   could say there are statutory issues here, someone

13   who could say there are constitutional issues

14   here. And none of that was litigated in those

15   FISA decisions.

16   And that was one reason why the court,

17   having not had the benefit of those arguments, may

18   have more easily approved the legality of the

19   program.

20   MS. WALD: And pointing out in the only

21   two cases where you had federal district court

22   judges, one said yes and one said no.

1   AUDIENCE MEMBER: And what does it say --

2   MR. MEDINE: Why don't we give somebody

3   else a chance --

4   MS. BRAND: No, I'm sorry, Pat, that's

5   actually not right. As a matter of statutory

6   construction, only one district judge has looked

7   at it as a matter of statutory construction and

8   has upheld it.

9   MS. WALD: Yes, I know, but the other one

10   denied constitutional --

11   MS. BRAND: It's not statutory --

12   MS. WALD: The other one denied

13   constitutional --

14   MS. BRAND: I'd also want to point out

15   that it's not as though opposing views are never

16   taken into account in the process of bringing a

17   position to the FISA court. There's extensive

18   quasi-adversarial briefing and debate and

19   argumentation inside the executive branch in what

20   used to be called OIPR, and it's now called

21   something else.

22   But it is not as though the FISA court is

1   an echo chamber. You know, the FISA court

2   consists of senate-confirmed regular district

3   judges sitting by designation on this court.

4   They take briefing. They can call on

5   third parties if they wish, although that has

6   rarely happened in the past, which is part of the

7   reason why we recommend beefing up that process.

8   But nothing reaches the FISA court unless it's

9   already been extensively vetted and debated within

10 the executive branch.

11   MS. COLLINS COOK: And one final point on

12 this question of the absence of an adversarial

13 process. I would direct you to our criminal

14 courts where search warrants and other types of

15 investigative process is routinely issued without

16 adversarial process.

17   That information or evidence obtained can

18 be tested if criminal charges are brought, just as

19 under the structure of FISA, to the extent that

20 information obtained pursuant to FISA is used

21 there is a use provision that information be

22 defended and the defendant must be notified of

1   that. And if criminal charges are brought, the

2   defendant would have the opportunity to challenge

3   the collection of that information.

4   MS. WALD: I just have to add something

5   to Beth's two points. In the first case,

6   virtually every time that a criminal subpoena is

7   issued there will be a chance down the line to

8   contest that, sometimes immediately, sometimes

9   when the evidence is actually entered because

10 you're in the middle of a criminal process.

11   The likelihood that a FISA thing will

12 eventuate in a criminal process is much, much

13 lower. I mean it's almost infinitesimal in terms

14 of the fact.

15   And secondly, it was only last year that

16 finally I think the interpretation was accepted

17 that, in fact, the government had to inform

18 somebody in a criminal division about the

19 derivative value or the derivative source of it.

20 So I don't think the two are comparable at all.

21   AUDIENCE MEMBER: Let me --

22   MR. MEDINE: You've had a lot of

1   questions.

2   AUDIENCE MEMBER: Yeah, I have two quick

3   questions. One is the notion that under your

4   legal analysis this program was never properly

5   statutorily authorized. What are the consequences

6   of that in practical terms?

7   The second is for Ms. Cook and Ms. Brand.

8   With regard to your comments on this being the

9   beginning of the conversation given the cyber

10   threats we face, I'd like to hear you expand on

11   that.

12   MR. MEDINE: Well, the consequences of

13   the legality is that the Board is recommending

14   that the program be terminated.

15   We understand, as courts often do, we're

16   not a court and so we don't make a final decision,

17   but that's our recommendation, that there is a

18   transition period to give the government a chance

19   with added privacy protections to transition to a

20   different program.

21   MR. DEMPSEY: The statute's a hundred

22   percent clear that the telephone companies, for

1   example, are not liable. They complied with a

2   court order and under the statute compliance with

3   a court order immunizes you against liability.

4   And we're saying that the government

5   officials acted in the best of intentions. But it

6   does happen, I mean Judge Wald has sat on

7   hundreds, if not thousands of cases literally

8   where she found, and other judges found, sometimes

9   after many, many years, that some governmental

10   action was not properly legally founded. And

11   that's what we are finding here, that's all. It's

12   time to push the reset button.

13   MS. COLLINS COOK: I'm happy to answer

14   the other part of the question. We are a new

15   Board. We have a mandate that directs us to

16   advise and conduct oversight with respect to

17   actions taken to protect the United States against

18   terror. That is part of what I meant by us being

19   at the beginning of the conversation.

20   We are just coming to maturity as a

21   Board, but we hope to be involved in conversations

22   about bulk collection in the future. And I would

1   note there are many who take the position that

2   cyber will require either access to or collection

3   of vast amounts of data.

4   AUDIENCE MEMBER: Thank you. Spencer

5   Ackerman (phonetic) with the Guardian.

6   Given your descriptions of the value of

7   the 215 program at its most expansive, even

8   considering the dissents, it seems to be more

9   prospective or ephemeral than it is in terms of

10   preventing an actual terrorist attack.

11   Do you feel that government officials

12   since the Snowden leaks began have been honest in

13   their presentation of the benefits to the public

14   with this program?

15   And for Ms. Cook and Ms. Brand, given

16   your skepticism that a private sector alternative

17   is workable and might, in fact, make the situation

18   worse, Ms. Brand sort of got into this a bit, do

19   you think there is really any alternative to

20   leaving the metadata collection with the NSA?

21   MS. BRAND: I wouldn't want to rule that

22   out. I mean I wouldn't think that my own

1   imagination represents the bounds of what's

2   possible, but I have not yet heard a proposal that

3   is better than keeping it with the NSA, with the

4   additional safeguards that we discussed. And

5   perhaps there are more safeguards that would

6   further protect privacy and still leave the

7   program operational.

8   But I don't think, I agree with Beth,

9   what Beth said earlier that a third party

10   alternative, something other than the service

11   providers that has been suggested, I don't see any

12   possible way that that could work.

13   And in terms of the providers themselves,

14   I think that just creates a whole host of legal

15   questions about the nature of the data,

16   responsibility for the data, liability of

17   companies, and additional privacy concerns. I

18   mean what if you want to get it for your divorce

19   proceeding, what's to keep you from subpoenaing

20   the provider?

21   I mean there are all kinds of questions

22   like that, that are raised and not answered

1   necessarily by transferring.

2   MS. WALD: Can I give a try at the first

3   part of your question?

4   AUDIENCE MEMBER: Please.

5   MS. WALD: It seems to me what you are

6   seeing is just a different philosophy, rather

7   than, at least it's my perception, rather than

8   somebody trying in the intelligence community to

9   mislead people as to the value of the program.

10   I think there's a sincere belief on the

11   part of many, and this is a value judgement which

12   I think the majority of us think needs to be made,

13   more so by the public than it has been in the

14   past, as to the way of it.

15   For instance, you know, we've heard

16   people describe, inside the intelligence community

17   say it's like fire insurance. You may never use

18   it but you ought to have the fire insurance on the

19   one out of, you know, a thousand chances that your

20   house is going to catch on fire, etcetera.

21   So this is, there's really a notion that

22   if something bad comes on down the line, or the

1   one in a hundred or thousand chances, that is a

2   value judgment, that it's worth collecting all of

3   this data with what some of us think down the line

4   could have a potential risk to privacy versus some

5   who think that the so-called, like, one percent,

6   one percent calculus is just not worth it. It's

7   really a balancing thing.

8   And I think some people, not all, some

9   people in the intelligence community think that it

10   is, and some of us think that it is not.

11   MR. MEDINE: Yes.

12   AUDIENCE MEMBER: Hi, Andrea Pierson

13   (phonetic) with the Washington Post. So actually

14   it's a little bit of a follow-up on Spencer's

15   question about third parties.

16   Generally that's how the question's been

17   interpreted in Obama's suggested changes to the

18   program. My understanding of what the three

19   members of this Board voting to, or recommending

20   that the program be terminated, and two of them

21   expressing severe concerns about the practicality

22   or possibility of that proposal working, that no

1   one on the board thinks that that's a very good

2   idea? Actually each of you individually speak to

3   that.

4   MR. DEMPSEY: I think the third party

5   idea is a terrible idea. It just replicates all

6   the problems that are unanswered, who is it, how

7   long do they keep it, who else gets it, how do

8   they secure it, what security requirements are

9   their employees subject to, who oversees it, is it

10   subject to the Constitution, where's the risk of

11   mission creep?

12   To me, you just take all the same

13   questions and you have to answer them all over

14   again from scratch. So I honestly do not see

15   that. It sounds to some people like an easy out.

16   It is not an easy out.

17   MS. WALD: I have a somewhat more

18   flexible attitude. So far people have just

19   talked, as I understand the review group, they had

20   no specific third parties that they were talking

21   about. I haven't heard anything come out.

22   I wouldn't knock down forever more the

1   notion that somebody somewhere could come up with

2   a scheme that made sense. I think for all the

3   reasons we don't have one now, and I wouldn't see

4   handing it over to somebody we manufactured for

5   the purposes.

6   The only person, and I'm joking, I'm not

7   saying seriously, but I had thought to myself, in

8   government, where is the only place I think you

9   could probably, you know, protect? And I kept

10   thinking, well, the Census Bureau is pretty good.

11   They have a lot of terrific information about

12   people, and so far as I know, they've never

13   (inaudible). That's a joke. That's not --

14   But other than that, I can't think of

15   anybody. But we are in such an early state in

16   this whole business about use and collection of

17   data that for me, I don't rule anything out

18   absolutely till we rule on specific proposals.

19   Not rule on, but.

20   MR. MEDINE: I would just add,

21   aggregating sensitive personal information for

22   hundreds of millions of Americans in one place

1   doesn't solve the problem that we're facing now of

2   having the government have access to that

3   information.

4   It's far better to access the information

5   on an as-needed basis where there's some

6   indication. We'd have to start by creating a

7   whole new legal structure for that, liability, and

8   it just doesn't seem to address the concerns that

9   we've raised.

10   Other questions?

11   AUDIENCE MEMBER: I had a question about

12   the Special Advocates program. How would that be

13   structured? Based on any (inaudible) programs?

14   How would the pool of adversaries be decided?

15   MR. MEDINE: I think it's a somewhat

16   novel approach, but what we tried to accomplish is

17   to have an outside voice in the court who could

18   address privacy and civil liberties concerns, not

19   somebody who's institutionalized as part of the

20   court or part of the executive branch but someone

21   who could independently come in to cases and

22   express the concerns of the type that could have

1   been raised about the 215 program in future cases

2   where broad programs are being adopted or novel

3   legal issues are being considered.

4   Our proposal is that the court would

5   choose from a panel of qualified attorneys who

6   have appropriate security clearances or are able

7   to get the security clearances.

8   The court would provide space for them to

9   work in a secure facility to handle classified

10   information, and that they would be part of the

11   cases and have an opportunity to raise objections

12   to the government's requests and ultimately to

13   request an appeal if the government's request is

14   approved.

15   Yes?

16   AUDIENCE MEMBER: Ray Thomas, Jr.,

17   Department of Commerce, Trademark Public Advisory

18   Committee.

19   Mr. Chairman, I have perhaps what will be

20   the easiest question of the afternoon. You all

21   are handing some very serious issues and so I can

22   only imagine how big the workload is. I heard at

1   least two Board members mention how thin your

2   staff is. And I know you're building the Agency,

3   and I also know that there was a job posting for

4   attorney advisors. If you're at liberty to say,

5   how many attorney advisors are you looking to

6   bring on and what's your time frame?

7   MR. MEDINE: Not really a press question,

8   but I will say that we're looking to hire three or

9   four people. We've received over a thousand

10 applications and we're about to dig into them.

11   But we have a tremendous small staff now

12 that has produced a voluminous report, but we are

13 hoping to ease the burden on them in the near

14 future by hiring people.

15   Let's take maybe two or three more

16 questions.

17   AUDIENCE MEMBER: I told you it would be

18 the easiest question.

19   AUDIENCE MEMBER: What do you think of

20 the President's recommendations?

21   MS. WALD: We like his FISC

22 recommendation because it's the same as ours,

62

1   basically. Ours is fleshed out.

2   AUDIENCE MEMBER: I mean did you think it

3   was insufficient in any way or it covered its

4   bases, or what?

5   MR. DEMPSEY: Well, two things. He

6   didn't answer the question of what does the new

7   program look like. He kicked that down the road.

8   And he, in my view, hasn't fully grappled

9   with the problem that the statute that's currently

10   on the books and that currently serves as the

11   basis for the program doesn't fit with the

12   problem, doesn't fit with the way the program is

13   being operated.

14   The President called for, said we need to

15   have a national debate on this question of how do

16   we collect large quantities of data. But it was

17   not clear whether he fully appreciated the need to

18   go back to some basics.

19   I think part of the speech made it sound

20   like you could add some additional protections to

21   the existing program and gloss over the

22   fundamental question.

1   The trouble with that is then what's the

2 next program, and the next program, and the next

3 program? Because once we say 215 is the basis for

4 bulk collection on this broad interpretation of

5 relevance and on this ongoing basis, I think

6 that's the fundamental question that really we've

7 never had a public debate about, and to leap over

8 that question I think is a mistake.

9   MS. WALD: There's no limiting principle

10 in it.

11   MS. BRAND: Jake, I just want to make

12 clear that the Board has no position on the

13 President's speech because -- other than I mean

14 we've addressed a couple of the subjects that were

15 the subjects of his speech but most of the

16 recommendations that he made touch on subjects we

17 have not studied as a Board.

18   We obviously have to operate by majority

19 vote after studying and so forth, and I as an

20 individual Board member wouldn't been ready to

21 opine on the subjects that we have not yet studied

22 without talking to the government and doing a lot

1   more study.

2   MR. MEDINE: All right, let's take one

3   more question from this press over here. Yes?

4   AUDIENCE MEMBER: Mr. Dempsey, you

5   mentioned a flaw in the congressional process

6   where there was a tacit agreement about how to

7   interpret this statute versus what was presented

8   publicly.

9   I wonder if you could just elaborate on

10   where that gap occurred, on Congress's side or on

11   the Agency's side, and if the rest of the panel

12   also saw that kind of problem.

13   MR. DEMPSEY: Well, the problem occurred

14   initially in 2005, 2006, when Congress was

15   debating the reauthorization of the PATRIOT Act,

16   Section 215, talked about it publicly as if it

17   were a particularized collection program for

18   individual records when, in fact, it knew that

19   there was a bulk collection program and that the

20   government was seeking to bring that under Section

21   215.

22   It was compounded when that provision

1   came up for sunset re-examination, I think in 2009

2   and 2011, and again Congress, by then at least the

3   intelligence committees and the judiciary

4   committees were fully aware of the program and

5   were fully aware that it was being conducted under

6   Section 215, but there was not a hint of that in

7   the public debate. And there's not a hint of

8   that, in my view, in the words of the statute.

9   And it was I think a mistake going to

10   democratic accountability for Congress to believe

11   it was blessing a program that could not be

12   discerned from a plain reading of the statute.

13   Now we concluded that their so-called

14   ratification or re-enactment was actually not

15   effective. You cannot cure, by Congress

16   re-passing a statute knowing how it's being

17   interpreted, you cannot bless that interpretation

18   and you cannot infuse that interpretation into the

19   statute if the interpretation is so contrary to

20   the words of the statute.

21   MR. MEDINE: Okay, thank you.

22   MS. COLLINS COOK: I'm sorry, I don't

66

1   think you asked whether or not the other Board

2   members agree that there was a flaw in the system.

3   I do not agree that there was a flaw in

4   the system. I think we live in a representative

5   democracy and I think our foundational document,

6   the Constitution, explicitly contemplates secret

7   proceedings. I'd direct you to Article 1 Section

8   5 of the Constitution.

9   I think that any requirement that would

10   require a detailed legislative discussion about

11   our most sensitive national security programs is

12   unworkable. We've never had that understanding.

13   I do not sign on to such an understanding.

14   MS. WALD: The constitutional basis, like

15   I say, is a debatable proposition, referring you

16   to the Federalist Papers.

17   MR. MEDINE: There is clearly a debate

18   but that will not continue here.

19   (Laughter)

20   (Whereupon, at 2:05 p.m., the meeting was

21   adjourned)

22

67

```
1                        CERTIFICATION

2

3

4          I, LYNNE LIVINGSTON, A Notary Public of

5   the State of Maryland, Baltimore County, do hereby

6   certify that the proceedings contained herein were

7   recorded by me stenographically; that this

8   transcript is a true record of the proceedings.

9          I further certify that I am not of

10  counsel to any of the parties, nor in any way

11  interested in the outcome of this action.

12         As witness my hand and notarial seal this

13  _____ day of _____, 2013.

14         _____

15         Lynne Livingston

16         Notary Public

17         My commission expires: December 10, 2014

18

19

20

21

22
```

A				
	54:4,17 62:20	afternoon 3:2	31:14 32:3,3,4	47:18 60:14
ability 42:11	address 46:22	60:20	32:6,9,14	approving 11:8
able 23:16 60:6	47:1 59:8,18	agencies 14:12	39:18 46:11,18	arena 31:11
absence 49:12	addressed 16:19	29:22	51:4	argumentation
absolutely 18:18	46:21 63:14	agency 5:17	analysts 42:11	48:19
29:4,4 58:18	adequate 35:16	22:2 36:15	Andrea 56:12	arguments 23:6
academics 5:20	37:10 40:14	61:2	announced 3:10	47:5,17
accept 17:8	42:19 43:1	Agency's 64:11	announcement	arises 21:17
accepted 50:16	47:7	aggregating	17:4	Article 66:7
access 5:1 6:1	adjourn 45:4,11	58:21	answer 20:5	articulable 10:6
53:2 59:2,4	45:15	agree 21:21	21:11 31:12	10:13
accompanying	adjourned	27:18 28:6	35:11 45:17	as-needed 59:5
29:13	45:15 66:21	29:14,16 31:2	52:13 57:13	asked 66:1
accomplish	adjourning	38:14 39:14	62:6	aspects 21:6
59:16	45:12	40:2 41:20	answered 20:6	assess 39:11
account 30:8	administration	54:8 66:2,3	54:22	assessing 18:15
48:16	43:4	agreement 28:4	anybody 25:1	42:3
accountability	administrations	64:6	25:12 26:18	assistance 12:15
65:10	25:17 38:21	agrees 24:13	28:14,15 58:15	associated 34:13
accuracy 6:9	adopt 4:1 43:3	akin 26:16	appeal 27:18	34:16 41:9
Ackerman 53:5	adopted 60:2	allow 34:2	30:5 60:13	associations
acquired 8:2	adopting 44:6	allowing 16:7	appeals 27:21	5:22
Act 1:6 4:3 8:20	44:10	allows 33:11,13	appear 10:18	assuaged 43:8
64:15	adoption 44:5	alternative 35:8	appellate 11:1	assume 15:5
acted 46:15 52:5	advantage 12:14	37:11 42:19	12:11	assured 29:8
action 33:5	adversarial	43:1,8,12	application 30:9	attack 37:20
52:10 67:11	49:12,16	53:16,19 54:10	applications	38:6 42:3,18
actions 52:17	adversaries	alternatives	10:20 26:20	53:10
activities 13:15	27:15 33:21	35:13	61:10	attention 14:8
45:3	34:3 59:14	Amendment	apply 20:10	attitude 57:18
actual 40:15	adversary 27:12	32:16,17	appreciate	attorney 12:22
41:16 42:21	27:17 47:9	American 39:1	29:10	13:13 61:4,5
53:10	advice 7:10	Americans	appreciated	attorneys 10:18
add 22:7 32:1	advise 7:6 52:16	11:18 13:20	62:17	27:5 60:5
47:8 50:4	advisors 61:4,5	15:3 28:12	appreciation	AUDIENCE
58:20 62:20	advisory 31:7	58:22	14:4	45:18 46:13
added 51:19	60:17	amount 35:17	approach 37:15	48:1 50:21
addition 41:10	advocate 10:17	amounts 34:10	43:6 59:16	51:2 53:4 55:4
additional 6:3	13:2 30:4,5	53:3	appropriate 5:2	56:12 59:11
9:21 10:21	47:11	analogy 18:10	10:11 60:6	60:16 61:17,19
12:5 17:9	advocates 5:20	18:12	appropriately	62:2 64:4
29:18 33:19	59:12	analysis 6:14,21	7:8	authorities 9:20
41:15 44:17,22	affect 28:12	7:3 15:14,16	approval 9:6	11:18 12:14
	affiliation 28:14	16:11,20 21:21	approved 46:8	13:20 22:21

33:19 34:8	63:3,5 66:14	31:6 36:12	19:11 30:22	**Chairman** 2:3
authority 18:12	**bear** 22:5	38:14 39:8	31:8 35:3	3:12 14:3,9
22:14	**beefing** 49:7	41:15 44:17,22	52:22 63:4	24:16 36:11
authorized 9:10	**began** 53:12	45:7 51:13	64:19	60:19
14:22 15:4	**beginning** 31:11	52:15,21 56:19	**burden** 61:13	**challenge** 50:2
21:19 22:3,11	51:9 52:19	57:1 61:1	**Bureau** 5:16	**chamber** 49:1
32:7 33:1	**belief** 55:10	63:12,17,20	58:10	**chance** 48:3
38:15 46:17	**believe** 4:19	66:1	**business** 58:16	50:7 51:18
51:5	18:11 19:4,6	**Board's** 6:19 7:1	**button** 52:12	**chances** 55:19
authorizes 8:1	22:13 29:19	7:3,5,13,16		56:1
8:15 38:17	31:18 33:10	32:14 36:18,21	**C**	**change** 25:17
availability 42:7	34:20 37:4	37:2 38:12	**calculate** 41:21	26:3
available 27:17	39:8 65:10	39:14 40:1,2	**calculus** 56:6	**changes** 6:20
35:18,19 36:18	**believed** 46:16	40:21 41:12	**call** 3:18 27:8	10:2 25:9,12
43:15 45:1,5	**believes** 7:21	44:2,5 45:3	34:13,16,17	32:15 37:5
avoid 42:13	11:17	**boils** 40:4	45:11 49:4	56:17
aware 15:16	**benefit** 19:22	**books** 62:10	**called** 16:8	**charges** 49:18
31:20 65:4,5	27:12 42:3,8	**bottom** 7:19	19:10 27:5	50:1
aye 3:19,20 44:7	47:17	**bounds** 54:1	48:20,20 62:14	**choose** 60:5
44:8,11,12,18	**benefits** 11:8	**branch** 4:22 7:7	**calling** 8:12	**cited** 15:21 46:6
44:19 45:12,13	31:1 53:13	14:11 17:5	**calls** 15:2	**citizens** 26:7
	best 18:18 31:12	48:19 49:10	**careful** 29:16	**civil** 1:1 3:3 4:15
B	46:19 52:5	59:20	**case** 9:8 21:2	5:5,20 7:7,20
back 11:10	**Beth** 29:5 41:6	**brand** 2:4 3:16	23:17 27:15	13:14 21:16
17:10 23:10	54:8,9	36:10,11,14	30:5 39:16	59:18
25:16 36:19	**Beth's** 50:5	48:4,11,14	50:5	**classification**
38:2,4 62:18	**better** 39:11	51:7 53:15,18	**cases** 10:19 22:1	6:20
background 5:3	54:3 59:4	53:21 63:11	23:9,12 24:8	**classified** 5:1
bad 15:6 55:22	**big** 18:9 25:4,18	**brief** 36:19	27:2,12 47:9	6:2,4 38:1 60:9
balancing 56:7	60:22	**briefing** 48:18	47:21 52:7	**clear** 41:22
Baltimore 67:5	**bit** 53:18 56:14	49:4	59:21 60:1,11	51:22 62:17
based 9:15	**blanket** 28:15	**briefings** 5:2,13	**catch** 55:20	63:12
10:13 26:21	**bless** 65:17	**briefly** 26:12	**caution** 30:18	**clearances** 60:6
35:5 44:1	**blessing** 65:11	**bring** 61:6 64:20	35:13	60:7
59:13	**blue** 22:9	**bringing** 48:16	**Census** 58:10	**clearly** 15:6
bases 62:4	**board** 1:1 2:1	**broad** 60:2 63:4	**Center** 1:15 3:7	66:17
basic 26:5,8	3:4,14,15 4:1,7	**broadly** 31:8	**Central** 5:17	**colleague's**
basically 26:4	5:6,18 6:1,8,10	**brought** 14:8	**certain** 8:22	35:10
62:1	6:14 7:14,21	17:15 49:18	13:9	**colleagues** 29:7
basics 62:18	9:7,9,16,20	50:1	**certainly** 19:19	**collect** 8:16 26:6
basis 9:14 11:7	10:1 11:16,22	**build** 25:19	22:16,21 24:17	41:4 62:16
15:15 18:9	13:14,16,22	**building** 61:2	**CERTIFICA...**	**collected** 8:5
22:22 23:20	14:5 15:18	**bulk** 8:6 12:3,6	67:1	34:14 40:16,18
59:5 62:11	20:18 21:7	14:22 17:8,11	**certify** 67:6,9	41:3

collecting 17:11
40:18 56:2
collection 8:4
15:1 17:9
18:10,13 19:12
25:6,7,8 26:9
30:10,22 31:8
35:4 40:9 50:3
52:22 53:2,20
58:16 63:4
64:17,19
Collins 2:7 29:6
49:11 52:13
65:22
combating
37:15
come 22:19 24:1
24:6 25:5,19
26:13 45:20
57:21 58:1
59:21
comes 28:11
55:22
coming 52:20
commencing
1:16
commend 29:7
commended
32:22
commending
36:12
comments 4:18
51:8
Commerce
60:17
commission
67:17
Committee
60:18
committees 65:3
65:4
communicate
15:7
communication

5:21 41:3
communicatio...
8:20 34:12
community 4:10
4:13 6:17 55:8
55:16 56:9
companies 5:21
8:11 13:6,8
19:17,20 35:19
43:13 51:22
54:17
comparable
50:20
complete 6:18
45:4
completely 28:4
compliance 20:9
52:2
complied 52:1
compliment
29:9
compounded
64:22
concept 17:21
17:22 18:8
concern 32:2
concerned 23:15
37:13
concerns 9:12
35:4,5,15,21
36:5 37:5,13
43:2,9,15
54:17 56:21
59:8,18,22
conclude 47:3,6
concluded 9:8
15:18 16:6
65:13
conclusion
31:22 39:15
40:3
conclusions
6:16 7:13,16
27:15

concur 36:21
conduct 52:16
conducted 1:5
4:2,7 15:13
16:5 65:5
confidence
29:20
confirming
33:20
Congress 12:7
12:10 17:4
18:17 23:4
30:1 33:5
64:14 65:2,10
65:15
Congress's 9:4
64:10
congressional
5:4 9:6 24:5
33:3 64:5
conjunction
33:18
connect 34:2
connection 8:3
connections
15:9 33:15
42:13
consensus 26:13
consent 3:22
44:21 45:14
consequences
51:5,12
consider 32:13
39:20
considered 7:8
9:3 31:21 39:4
60:3
considering
23:5 42:16
53:8
consistent 6:6
12:18 21:15
30:20
consists 49:2

Constitution
57:10 66:6,8
constitutional
9:11,15 22:20
22:20 23:6,22
30:14 31:15
32:14 39:16
47:13 48:10,13
66:14
constitutional...
22:18 39:14
construction
48:6,7
contact 28:14
contained 67:6
contemplates
66:6
content 28:17
34:11,18 41:3
contest 50:8
contextual 32:4
continue 9:13
40:4 66:18
continues 41:1
contrary 65:19
contribute
37:17 39:9
contribution
24:5
control 26:4
controls 25:22
26:1,2
controversial
21:6 32:21
controversy
26:19
convened 4:1
conversation
51:9 52:19
conversations
52:21
convinced 22:16
Cook 2:7 3:16
29:5,6 49:11

51:7 52:13
53:15 65:22
cooperation
4:22 14:11
copy 6:10
core 27:4 40:1
cornerstone
32:5
correct 6:18
corrective 33:5
counsel 67:10
counterterror...
15:11 34:7
38:3
counting 35:15
country 4:14
County 67:5
couple 25:16
63:14
course 4:17 14:6
39:19
court 1:8 4:5 5:8
5:13 6:12,12
10:9,10,16
11:3,3 12:8,9
12:13,20 14:22
17:5 22:1
23:15 24:20
26:13,17 27:14
27:20,22 29:17
30:6,14 33:4
39:5,6,16 44:4
46:1,7 47:16
47:21 48:17,22
49:1,3,8 51:16
52:2,3 59:17
59:20 60:4,8
court's 11:8
12:12 15:4
courts 39:10
49:14 51:15
covered 62:3
craft 38:10
create 43:14

created 19:18
19:21
creates 40:19
54:14
creating 59:6
creation 10:16
creep 29:2 57:11
criminal 49:13
49:18 50:1,6
50:10,12,18
criteria 13:17
26:22
critical 15:10
42:14
criticism 14:15
culture 28:9
cure 65:15
current 9:17
10:4 20:15
currently 62:9
62:10
custody 43:5
customers 35:21
cyber 31:10
51:9 53:2

D
D.C 1:16 3:8
danger 25:3
dangerous
40:13
data 15:6 17:12
18:9 19:16,21
19:22 30:22
31:8 34:10,11
36:1,9 40:19
42:6,16 43:5
43:13,15 53:3
54:15,16 56:3
58:17 62:16
databanks 26:7
database 10:14
date 3:4 35:14
David 2:3

day 14:13 16:18
45:3 67:13
deadline 9:4
dealt 23:12 24:8
debatable 66:15
debate 17:6 19:9
19:10 20:16,19
28:20 41:6
48:18 62:15
63:7 65:7
66:17
debated 49:9
debating 64:15
decades 25:16
December 7:13
67:17
decent 17:14
decided 59:14
decision 51:16
decisions 11:2,7
11:11,15 12:12
12:19,20 24:20
45:19 47:15
declassification
11:6
declassify 12:20
declassifying
11:11,14
dedicated 4:12
4:14
defendant 49:22
50:2
defended 49:22
defenders 18:3
26:16
demand 38:7
demands 38:2
democracy 66:5
democratic
65:10
demonstrated
9:12
Dempsey 2:6
3:16 14:2,3

45:22 46:15
51:21 57:4
62:5 64:4,13
denied 48:10,12
Department
5:15 60:17
depend 23:8
derivative 50:19
50:19
describe 55:16
description 6:11
descriptions
53:6
designation
49:3
designed 17:1
desirable 16:3
desire 14:18
despite 17:13
detail 22:14
detailed 66:10
details 28:19
29:1
determinations
10:7,7
determine 10:10
determined
11:19
detrimental
25:11
develop 13:8
developing
13:17
development
7:8 31:5
different 19:5,7
33:7 38:22
51:20 55:6
differentiation
25:6
difficult 38:17
43:17
dig 19:8 61:10
direct 49:13

66:7
direction 38:5
directly 9:19
Director 5:14
directs 52:15
discerned 65:12
disclose 13:9
disconnect 16:4
disconnects 47:1
discontinued
9:17
discretion 30:6
discuss 7:12
22:13 41:13
discussed 22:13
54:4
discussion 4:6
22:8 24:1,12
25:2 31:12,15
66:10
dismiss 33:14
disrupt 15:10
dissent 37:7,12
dissenters 21:7
dissenting 38:11
dissents 24:14
53:8
district 27:14
39:6 47:21
48:6 49:2
divide 46:3
division 50:18
divorce 54:18
document 66:5
documents 6:4
doing 10:5
33:12 63:22
domestic 15:1
dots 34:2
doubt 38:5 43:6
draft 6:10,14
drawn 10:17
duty 7:5
dynamic 38:9

E
earlier 54:9
early 41:7 58:15
ease 61:13
easiest 60:20
61:18
easily 47:18
easy 20:2 36:15
41:21 57:15,16
echo 35:9 49:1
effective 15:5
43:8,11 65:15
effectively 13:4
effectiveness 6:5
9:13 18:3,15
efficacy 6:15
31:15 33:8
effort 32:20
efforts 29:21
38:3
Eight 12:22
either 19:17
31:14 35:1
40:3 43:10
53:2
elaborate 64:9
elaborated 23:7
Electronic 8:19
elements 7:6
19:1
Eleven 13:16
Elisebeth 2:7
3:16
emerged 19:15
emphasize 4:11
24:15
emphasizes 25:3
employees 57:9
enabling 12:8
enact 12:7,10
encompassing
8:6
encourages 45:7

ended 16:7	51:10	facts 34:19	29:17 39:5	27:6,6 52:8,8
enforce 20:8	expanded 17:20	factual 6:17	46:1,7 47:9,15	foundation 47:7
enhance 7:11	expanding	fades 37:22	48:17,22 49:1	foundational
ensure 6:9,17	10:22	failing 37:21	49:8,19,20	66:5
7:7 13:3	expansive 53:7	fairly 21:17	50:11	founded 52:10
entered 50:9	expedite 27:22	faith 4:20 32:20	FISC 5:19 6:2	four 61:9
entity 19:16	expert 27:4	38:21	10:9,10,18	Fourth 8:15
ephemeral 53:9	experts 23:19	falling 16:2	11:1,7,11 13:7	12:10 32:16
equation 41:18	25:8	far 16:2 31:20	24:20 26:13,17	frame 11:14
equipped 39:11	expiration 9:5	57:18 58:12	27:7,19 28:7	61:6
equivalent 36:8	expire 20:15	59:4	61:21	framework
especially 42:20	expires 67:17	fast-breaking	fit 16:16 62:11	28:18 29:19
essentially 15:2	explain 34:6	30:12	62:12	36:7
establish 42:13	explaining	favor 3:19 44:6	five 3:14 10:4	fulfill 31:7
establishing	16:16	44:9,16 45:12	24:10	full 7:14 12:13
37:10	explicit 28:16	FBI 8:4,9,16	flaw 64:5 66:2,3	14:10 44:16,21
etcetera 20:10	explicitly 66:6	federal 3:11	flawed 17:18	fuller 34:2
25:18 55:20	exploit 24:22	5:16 16:13	18:20	fully 42:9 62:8
evaluate 34:6	express 14:1,4	31:20 33:1	fleshed 62:1	62:17 65:4,5
event 39:3	29:11 59:22	36:15 39:4	flexible 57:18	functional 36:8
events 30:12	expressing	47:21	focus 33:12	fundamental
eventuate 50:12	56:21	Federalist 66:16	focused 11:4	17:11 62:22
everybody	extension 9:4	feel 53:11	32:15	63:6
24:11,13	extensive 4:21	fewer 35:9	follow 5:10 24:4	furnish 8:11
evidence 4:16	48:17	field 25:19	follow-up 56:14	further 54:6
24:17 42:16	extensively 4:9	Fifth 12:13	Foreign 1:8 4:4	67:9
49:17 50:9	49:9	final 45:1 49:11	6:11 10:15	futile 42:14
exactly 23:11	extent 12:17	51:16	11:2 12:8 44:3	future 28:9
examined 16:13	30:19 49:19	finally 9:3 18:17	forever 57:22	52:22 60:1
example 32:1	extreme 26:14	28:2 50:16	forgotten 27:11	61:14
52:1		find 10:21 15:8	form 9:17 47:10	
exception 9:1	**F**	15:9	formally 4:1	**G**
exceptions 9:1	face 11:19 22:9	finding 52:11	former 5:19	gap 64:10
executive 4:22	42:9 51:10	fine 14:13	27:1	General 6:3
7:6 14:11 17:5	faced 16:4 18:2	fingers 37:21	forth 29:11	12:22 13:13
33:2 48:19	30:13	fire 55:17,18,20	63:19	Generally 56:16
49:10 59:20	facility 60:9	first 8:2 10:2	forums 6:8	George 1:14 3:6
exhaustive	facing 59:1	12:2 14:21	23:20	get-go 20:2
15:14	fact 10:9 14:16	21:4 29:16	forward 9:18	getting 36:13
exist 32:18	14:22 19:3	31:18 32:16	11:6 20:19	give 7:19 13:22
existing 8:13	22:7 23:4,8,15	37:13 38:14	30:1	29:9 48:2
12:14 22:21	25:9 50:14,17	50:5 55:2	found 4:11,16	51:18 55:2
62:21	53:17 64:18	FISA 5:8,13	14:17 15:17	given 16:6 17:3
expand 12:11,15	factor 42:2	13:7,15 14:22	16:14 24:17,19	17:9 30:5,5,21

31:9 34:19
51:9 53:6,15
gives 37:14
40:10
global 23:13
gloss 62:21
go 11:21 17:10
21:20 23:10
25:16 34:9
62:18
goal 14:20
going 9:18 11:6
11:10,21 22:11
23:4 24:7 25:4
28:10,12,15
30:1 38:4
55:20 65:9
good 3:2 4:20
26:2,14 32:20
38:20 39:22
57:1 58:10
gotten 41:6
governing 39:16
government
8:22 11:5 12:2
12:4,18 13:5
13:16 20:5
25:10 26:6
34:5 36:8
37:21 38:2,8
39:19 40:11
41:2 43:3 47:5
47:10 50:17
51:18 52:4
53:11 58:8
59:2 63:22
64:20
government's
13:10,15 38:19
60:12,13
governmental
52:9
grand 18:10
grant 38:18

grappled 62:8
greater 28:6
grounds 8:1
group 4:12
28:12 57:19
Guardian 53:5
guys 15:6

H

hand 23:3 40:9
41:2 67:12
handing 58:4
60:21
handle 60:9
handles 26:17
26:18
hands 40:13
happen 52:6
happened 49:6
happens 42:10
happy 52:13
hard 14:6 18:19
35:20
harm 33:13
hear 12:9 51:10
heard 14:21
23:19 54:2
55:15 57:21
60:22
hearing 3:18
held 1:14 6:8
19:16
help 15:10 35:21
helpful 10:21
Hi 56:12
highest 17:13
29:9
highly 16:2
hint 65:6,7
hire 61:8
hiring 61:14
history 22:9
27:19
hold 19:20,21

20:5 35:16
43:13
holding 36:8
hole 19:9
homeland 33:14
honest 25:14
53:12
honestly 57:14
hope 24:5 29:22
37:16 52:21
hoping 61:13
hops 10:4,5
host 43:17 54:14
house 5:18 7:12
55:20
huge 28:12
hundred 51:21
56:1
hundreds 26:19
52:7 58:22

I

idea 19:15,19
22:10 57:2,5,5
ideal 31:6
ideas 19:14
identified 16:19
43:2 47:1
identify 33:19
identifying 41:5
identities 34:15
34:18
identity 34:12
illegally 46:14
imagination
54:1
imagine 60:22
immediate 10:2
42:7
immediately
12:4 37:3
40:22 50:8
immovable
15:19

immunizes 52:3
imperative 30:8
implement 12:5
30:1
implementation
7:9
implemented
21:14,18 30:19
implications
32:17
importance
30:11
important 20:1
21:1,12 22:12
23:4 28:3,8
importantly
37:2
impose 36:1
imposing 9:21
in-depth 5:6
15:15
inadvertent
24:19
inaudible 45:20
58:13 59:13
include 34:11,12
included 5:13
36:17
including 27:18
31:10 37:8
incomplete
46:19
inconsistent
7:22
increase 29:19
increasing 31:10
indefinitely
23:16
independence
7:2
independent
12:9
independently
59:21

indicated 9:6
29:14 33:17
indication 7:1
59:6
individual 7:17
13:22 24:9
26:20,20 45:4
63:20 64:18
individually
57:2
individuals 4:19
34:13,16
infinitesimal
50:13
inform 13:13
50:17
information
8:16,18,21
13:1,10 15:1
15:11 23:21
25:1,7,10
28:16 33:20
35:17 36:6
38:1 40:12,16
40:18 41:5
49:17,20,21
50:3 58:11,21
59:3,4 60:10
informative
28:17
infuse 65:18
initial 15:3
initially 64:14
input 12:16
inside 48:19
55:16
Inspector 6:3
instance 55:15
instances 29:3
institution
26:15
institutional
39:7
institutionaliz...

59:19
instruments
23:13
insufficient
37:14 62:3
insurance 55:17
55:18
intelligence 1:8
4:4,9,13 5:15
5:17 6:12,17
10:15 11:2
12:8 14:12
30:10 44:4
55:8,16 56:9
65:3
intended 14:15
17:22
intentional
24:18
intentions 18:19
52:5
interact 4:9
interested 45:7
67:11
interests 40:5
41:17 42:22
international
15:2
Internet 13:6
interpret 64:7
interpretation
31:19 32:11
38:19 50:16
63:4 65:17,18
65:19
interpreted
56:17 65:17
Interruption 3:9
intimidate 24:22
intrusion 40:5
40:20 41:16
42:21
investigation
4:17 8:4,8,9

investigations
5:16 32:5,7,9
investigative
49:15
investigators
33:11,14
invited 10:18
involve 34:10
involved 52:21
involves 11:12
involving 10:19
issue 16:14
44:21
issued 46:16
49:15 50:7
issues 30:15
37:19 47:12,13
60:3,21
issuing 44:16
46:1

J

Jake 63:11
James 2:6 3:16
January 1:10
3:5,11 7:14
Jim 27:9
job 61:3
join 30:3,16
31:13 37:2
39:17
joined 35:5
40:21
joke 58:13
joking 58:6
Jones 23:12
journey 20:13
Jr 60:16
judge 5:19
10:20 16:18
20:21 24:3
31:20 39:4
48:6 52:6
judgement

55:11
judges 10:19
16:11,13 27:1
27:1,7,10,11
27:14 30:14
33:1 45:18
46:1,6,7,10,11
46:15,21 47:4
47:22 49:3
52:8
judgment 56:2
judicial 32:21
33:2
judiciary 65:3
June 5:4 14:21
jurisprudence
29:3 32:16
jury 18:10
Justice 5:15
justified 18:4
justifies 10:8

K

keep 14:14
18:19 54:19
57:7
keeping 13:11
36:4 54:3
kept 10:3 11:13
58:9
key 42:2,17
kicked 62:7
kind 23:21
24:17 25:19
26:21 27:2
29:2 64:12
kinds 25:22
54:21
knew 64:18
knock 57:22
know 18:6 21:5
22:15 38:7
48:9 49:1
55:15,19 58:9

58:12 61:2,3
knowing 65:16

L

laid 46:11
language 38:16
large 38:6 43:16
62:16
large-scale
42:10
Laughter 66:19
law 14:18 21:15
21:17 22:22
23:1,5,22 24:7
28:10,11,18
29:2 39:17
lawyers 47:5
layer 17:9
lead 19:6
leads 33:19
42:14
leak 38:1
leaks 16:15 46:9
46:20 53:12
leap 63:7
leave 43:20 54:6
leaving 53:20
led 19:3
left 30:6
legal 9:15,20
11:17 12:16
15:4 16:14
17:12 29:18
31:14 35:1
39:9 46:11,18
51:4 54:14
59:7 60:3
legality 21:4,9
22:13 47:18
51:13
legally 52:10
legislation 7:9
12:7,10 24:6
legislative 22:9

32:22 66:10
length 46:4
let's 61:15 64:2
liability 20:9
52:3 54:16
59:7
liable 52:1
liberties 1:1 3:3
5:5,20 7:7,21
13:14 21:16
59:18
liberty 61:4
light 23:11
39:18 42:20
likelihood 50:11
likewise 32:11
limit 18:11
limitations
41:11
limited 16:2,6
limiting 17:22
63:9
limits 30:13
line 7:19 50:7
55:22 56:3
literally 41:8
52:7
litigated 47:14
little 41:20
56:14
live 14:18 66:4
Livingston 1:20
67:4,15
located 3:7
location 23:13
logical 15:5,8
long 20:7,13
57:7
longer 43:13
longer-term
42:5
look 17:7 20:18
21:13 32:5
62:7

open 3:3
opening 3:19
operate 4:18,19
   6:7 39:20
   63:18
operated 4:20
   62:13
operates 8:10
   41:10
operating 12:6
operation 6:4
   9:6,13 13:2
   35:6 44:3
operational
   28:19,22 37:6
   54:7
operations 1:7
   4:4 5:8 6:11
   11:5 31:3
opine 63:21
opinion 16:16
   19:11 23:19
   43:19 46:10
opinions 6:2
   27:10 45:19
opponents
   16:21
opportunities
   11:1 12:11,15
opportunity 4:8
   14:1 29:10
   31:6 50:2
   60:11
opposed 8:12
   44:13
opposing 48:15
opposite 27:14
order 3:18 6:9
   52:2,3
orders 13:8
   20:15 46:2,16
ought 55:18
outcome 16:3
   67:11

outside 7:2
   12:16 59:17
outweighed
   40:6
over-read 22:2
overarching
   37:13
overhaul 23:5
oversees 20:9
   57:9
oversight 1:1
   3:4 5:6 7:21
   13:14 32:22
   33:3 40:14
   52:16
overwhelming
   16:4

P

p.m 1:17 3:4
   66:20
pages 21:3
paint 34:2
panel 10:17 60:5
   64:11
Papers 66:16
paraphrasing
   21:22
part 6:6 27:7
   37:12 49:6
   52:14,18 55:3
   55:11 59:19,20
   60:10 62:19
participating
   20:19
participation
   30:4
particular 7:11
   8:8 11:9 43:6
particularized
   26:21 64:17
parties 12:16
   38:22 45:8
   49:5 56:15

57:20 67:10
parts 28:6
party 19:18,21
   36:5 43:5 54:9
   57:4
passed 28:10,11
Pat 48:4
Patricia 2:5
   3:16
PATRIOT 1:6
   4:3 64:15
pause 40:10
PCLOB 7:11
pclob.gov 45:1,8
   45:10
peace 18:5,14
pendulum 37:17
   38:4
people 14:13
   17:14 22:15
   24:21 25:14
   28:21 39:1
   55:9,16 56:8,9
   57:15,18 58:12
   61:9,14
perceived 27:6
percent 51:22
   56:5,6
perception 55:7
period 16:8
   24:10 51:18
permanent 9:14
permissible
   31:19
permitted 10:5
permitting 13:8
person 25:15
   58:6
personal 58:21
personally 41:4
philosophy 55:6
phone 15:2
   19:20
phonetic 53:5

56:13
phrase 29:8
   45:19
pick 20:22
picture 34:3
pieces 21:1
Pierson 56:12
place 41:14
   42:20 58:8,22
plain 19:5 65:12
plan 43:4
please 44:7,11
   44:17 55:4
pleased 20:11
   36:22
plot 42:10,15
plots 15:10
   33:15
plucky 29:7,9
point 13:22
   16:21 23:12
   28:2 32:2
   48:14 49:11
pointed 24:16
pointing 47:20
points 26:11
   37:21 50:5
policies 7:9
policy 9:15
   17:17 18:8
   21:10 24:12
   35:1 38:10
   39:12,22
policy-making
   37:18
politically 24:22
pool 59:14
poses 34:21 35:9
   36:2
posing 30:12
position 48:17
   53:1 63:12
possesses 40:11
possibility 56:22

possible 6:8
   12:17 25:17
   30:19 54:2,12
Post 56:13
posted 45:10
posting 61:3
potential 25:3
   25:13 30:21
   31:1 32:15
   33:14 40:5
   56:4
potentially 8:6
   32:20 36:2
power 7:11
   25:12
practical 51:6
practicality
   56:21
precedent 23:1
   23:11
precious 42:13
present 3:14
   7:16
presentation
   53:13
presented 47:5
   64:7
President 7:6,15
   7:15 16:8
   19:10 20:13
   62:14
President's 7:17
   17:3 61:20
   63:13
presidential 5:4
presiding 3:12
   5:19
press 45:6 61:7
   64:3
pressed 35:20
pressure 17:14
   36:1
pretty 58:10
prevent 37:22

reason 22:17 24:14 32:10 47:16 49:7	recommends 10:1 41:16	46:5	30:11	safeguards 12:5 41:11,14,15 54:4,5
reasonable 10:6 10:13 38:20	record 10:5 19:2 19:3 28:20 45:16 67:8	replicates 57:5 reply 25:21 report 1:4 3:19	response 5:3 responsibility 39:1 54:16	sat 52:6 saw 64:12
reasoning 11:8	recorded 67:7	4:2,7 5:9 6:10	responsible 30:2	saying 20:4
reasons 9:16 21:20 35:2 38:11 58:3	records 1:4 4:2 8:2,5,7,12,14 10:3,8,11 12:3	6:19 7:20 12:1 13:1 14:14,16 21:2,6 29:13 29:15 36:13,18	rest 36:12 64:11 restricts 8:20 rests 31:18 result 22:19	22:19 24:2 46:6,18 52:4 58:7 says 22:2
reauthorization 64:15	34:14,17,17 35:16 36:4	37:14,16 41:12 44:6,6,10,16	35:22 resulting 6:21	scale 30:22 31:9 38:6 40:9
reauthorized 33:6	42:11 44:2 64:18	44:21,22 45:8 61:12	results 15:17 16:1,6 18:5	scan 42:11 scheme 58:2
receive 13:7	reduce 37:5	Report's 37:8	37:12	scope 11:17
received 4:21 14:9,10 61:9	reduces 43:2 referring 66:15	Reported 1:20 reports 6:3	retain 7:10 retention 9:21	13:19 18:11 scratch 57:14
receives 8:17	reflected 19:1	representative	36:1	seal 67:12
receiving 3:21 44:20	regard 35:12 51:8	66:4 represented	revealing 40:10 review 6:20 7:2	search 10:8 49:14
recognize 20:1 20:12	regarded 8:7 regarding 13:2	32:19 represents 54:1	10:10 11:1,3 12:11 27:22	searches 10:6,11 10:12
recognized 30:7	regime 29:2	request 60:13	44:2 45:8	second 8:5 12:4
recognizing 11:12	Register 3:11 regular 39:6	60:13 requested 5:2	57:19 right 18:9,12,15	30:21 37:16 51:7
recommend 9:16,21 10:16	49:2 regularly 13:1,7	requests 5:4 13:10 60:12	22:22 48:5 64:2	secondly 16:1 50:15
10:22 11:6,10 42:18 49:7	relating 6:4 relative 34:7	require 53:2 66:10	rights 4:15 risk 30:12 34:21	secrecy 30:8 secret 29:2 66:6
recommendat... 24:2 30:3,17	relatively 42:21 release 12:19	required 19:20 requirement	40:19 56:4 57:10	section 1:5 4:3 5:7,7,9 6:15
31:16 37:9 38:12 40:22	released 24:20 relevance 18:9	8:13 36:2 66:9 requirements	risks 30:21 35:9 road 25:13 62:7	19:4 22:18 28:5 31:4,17
51:17 61:22	32:3,6,11 63:5	9:22 57:8	role 31:7	33:9,11,18
recommendat... 6:16,22 7:4	relevant 8:8 17:19 22:5	requires 42:4 requiring 43:12	room 1:15 3:7 17:6 25:16	34:1 37:4,9 38:13,16 44:3
11:22 29:15,16 30:2,7,17 31:3	remarkably 14:6 41:11	reset 52:12 resolve 20:14,17	36:19 routinely 49:15	64:16,20 65:6 66:7
35:6 36:22 37:3,8 44:5,7	Remember 27:9 renewal 46:1	resolved 39:10 resource 30:13	rule 53:21 58:17 58:18,19	sector 53:16 secure 57:8 60:9
44:10 61:20 63:16	renewed 46:5 repeat 34:15	resources 11:12 respect 17:13	rules 13:8	security 12:18 13:12 14:19
recommending 47:11 51:13	41:13 repeated 46:1	29:17 47:3,4 52:16	**S** sacrificing 37:6	20:8 28:22 29:20 30:13,20
56:19	repeatedly 33:6	responding	safe 14:14 18:20	

36:6 37:19	severe 30:12	59:15	34:4 36:17	studying 15:12
38:10 40:6	56:21	sorry 12:21	41:13	63:19
41:19 43:17	shaped 17:16	16:12 28:4	statements 6:13	stuff 25:15
57:8 60:6,7	shoe-horned	48:4 65:22	6:18 44:17,22	subject 6:19
66:11	17:1	sort 53:18	States 24:11	10:12 21:7
see 19:22 31:10	short 16:2 29:12	sound 35:12	33:13 38:7	32:20 33:2
35:20 39:17	36:16	39:12 62:19	52:17	57:9,10
45:21 54:11	shut 31:16 34:22	sounds 57:15	station 20:12	subjects 63:14
57:14 58:3	37:9 38:12	source 50:19	statistic 27:9	63:15,16,21
seeing 45:21	shutting 42:19	space 60:8	statistical 13:9	subpoena 17:21
55:6	side 41:18 64:10	speak 57:2	statute 7:22	18:10 50:6
seeking 64:20	64:11	Special 10:17	8:15 9:11	subpoenaing
seeks 26:6	sign 66:13	13:2 30:4	15:21 16:5,17	54:19
seen 32:10,12	significant	47:10 59:12	17:1,15 19:6	substance 7:3
senate-confir...	10:19 11:11,12	specific 8:3,22	21:13 22:2,3	substitute 35:17
49:2	36:1	11:22 57:20	31:19 32:4	sufficient 9:13
senior 7:12,15	Similarly 30:16	58:18	34:20 38:20	36:6
sense 43:7 58:2	36:4	Specifically	46:12,21 47:2	suggested 25:8
sensitive 30:10	simple 35:10,11	30:3	47:6 52:2 62:9	54:11 56:17
58:21 66:11	simply 22:5	speculative	64:7 65:8,12	suggesting
sent 34:17	sincere 55:10	32:14	65:16,19,20	24:21 46:14
separate 29:12	single 39:4	speech 7:17	statute's 8:12	summarizing
34:4 36:16	sitting 49:3	62:19 63:13,15	51:21	36:20
41:12	situation 53:17	speed 30:11	statutes 11:20	sunset 65:1
series 9:11	situations 24:9	Spencer 53:4	statutorily	supplemental
serious 31:9	six 14:7	Spencer's 56:14	38:15 51:5	33:20
36:5 40:20	Sixth 12:17	spent 16:10	statutory 6:7	supply 33:20
60:21	skeptical 43:9	spirit 14:17	7:5 15:14	support 15:22
seriously 34:6	skepticism	squarely 40:1	16:11,20 26:21	35:8 43:6
38:22 39:19	53:16	staff 5:19 6:12	31:7,14 32:8,8	Supreme 11:3
58:7	small 41:17	7:12,12,15	39:5 47:12	22:1 23:14
servants 14:17	42:21 61:11	14:6 15:13	48:5,7,11	39:16
served 43:8	Smith 23:9	29:8 36:13	stenographica...	surveillance 1:8
serves 62:10	Snowden 16:15	61:2,11	67:7	4:5 6:12 10:15
service 13:6	46:9 53:12	stand 24:7	stick 21:9	11:2,17 12:9
42:12 43:21	so-called 56:5	standard 18:14	Street 1:16 3:8	13:19 44:4
54:10	65:13	18:15 19:12	strict 41:11	suspicion 10:6
Session 45:17	solve 59:1	20:7	structure 25:12	10:13 28:13
set 24:14 29:11	somebody 20:4	standards 17:12	49:19 59:7	swings 37:17
36:14	48:2 50:18	stands 32:10	structured	system 41:8
seven 14:7 16:12	55:8 58:1,4	start 36:12 59:6	59:13	66:2,4
16:13 17:17	59:19	starting 4:6 40:8	studied 63:17,21	
Seventeen 45:18	someday 18:7	state 58:15 67:5	study 4:8 5:6,12	**T**
seventh 12:21	somewhat 57:17	statement 29:12	6:6 64:1	tacit 64:6

take 12:13 30:8 33:7 38:22 46:2 49:4 53:1 57:12 61:15 64:2	tested 49:18	Thirty-eight 16:11	51:18,19	45:14
	thank 14:3 20:21 29:6 36:9,11 43:22 44:1 53:4 65:21	Thomas 60:16	transparency 11:4 13:18 28:5,7 29:18 30:16	unanimously 10:1,16
taken 33:6 48:16 52:17	theoretically 40:12	thought 26:16 27:4 58:7		unanswered 57:6
takes 9:9		thousand 55:19 56:1 61:9	tremendous 61:11	unauthorized 38:1
talk 45:6	thin 61:1	thousands 52:7	trends 23:6	unclassified 5:10
talked 57:19 64:16	thing 19:14 24:15 25:20 50:11 56:7	threats 31:10 33:10,15 36:2 51:10	triage 33:11	unconstitutio... 24:3
talking 57:20 63:22	things 15:19 21:2 25:9 28:3 62:5	three 10:3,5 44:15 56:18 61:8,15	tried 59:16	undergird 23:1
task 36:15			trouble 63:1	underlying 25:4
technical 12:15	think 17:8,17 20:1,15 21:1,4 21:11,12,16 22:12,18 23:3 23:7,22 24:4,7 24:13,15 25:2 25:3,21 26:5,9 26:12,13 27:16 27:22 28:3,6,8 29:1 32:19 34:5 35:22 41:16 43:11 46:2,13 50:16 50:20 53:19,22 54:8,14 55:10 55:12,12 56:3 56:5,8,9,10 57:4 58:2,8,14 59:15 61:19 62:2,19 63:5,8 65:1,9 66:1,4,5 66:9	thwarting 42:2 42:15	true 40:17 67:8	understand 51:15 57:19
techniques 30:10		till 58:18	try 36:19 55:2	understanding 18:21 34:20 56:18 66:12,13
technology 5:21		time 8:4 11:14 16:10 35:19 42:12,14 45:15 50:6 52:12 61:6	trying 55:8	
telephone 1:4 4:2 8:2,6,11,16 8:21 9:18 12:3 19:17 23:18 24:10 43:12,21 44:2 51:22			Turning 38:11 39:13	undertook 5:6
		times 16:12 45:22 46:8	turns 21:18	undetectable 15:9
		tinker 26:3	twelve 11:21 13:19 17:16 27:2 29:15	unfortunate 38:9
telephones 15:7		tiny 14:6 36:13	twenty 23:10,10	United 24:11 33:13 38:7 52:17
tells 32:4		today 4:1 20:11	twenty-five 23:10	
ten 13:13 27:1 29:14		today's 33:9 45:9	two 4:8 5:12 6:8 9:5 10:4 15:19 15:19 19:14 21:6 26:11 27:12,21 37:7 37:12 38:21 44:15 47:21 50:5,20 51:2 56:20 61:1,15 62:5	University 1:15 3:6
tentative 7:13		token 32:13		unknown 42:2
terminated 51:14 56:20		told 26:22 61:17		unknowns 15:8
terms 11:13 50:13 51:6 53:9 54:13		tool 33:10		unnecessary 32:15
		touch 63:16		unworkable 66:12
terrible 57:5		touchstone 32:8	type 59:22	upheld 39:3 48:8
terrific 58:11		track 23:16	types 34:21 49:14	uphold 45:20
terror 33:15 52:18		trade 5:21		urge 34:5
	thinking 58:10	Trademark 60:17	**U**	urges 13:16
terrorism 37:15 39:2	thinks 57:1	transcript 45:9 67:8	U.S 39:6	USA 1:6 4:3
terrorist 37:20 38:6 42:3,10 42:18 53:10	third 8:10 12:7 19:18,21 36:4 43:5 49:5 54:9 56:15 57:4,20	transfer 43:5,21	ultimate 39:15	use 15:6 25:6,11 25:20 26:1,1,2 26:4 28:11 49:21 55:17
		transferring 55:1	ultimately 60:12	
			unanimous 3:21 30:2 35:6 37:1 44:9,20,21	
test 41:22 42:1	thirty 27:20,21	transition 16:8		

58:16	20:21,22 47:20	went 18:18	year 5:5 50:15	**23** 1:10
usefulness 42:8	48:9,12 50:4	**whatsoever** 22:8	**years** 10:3,4	**237** 21:3
uses 24:19	52:6 55:2,5	**White** 5:18 7:12	16:12,13 17:16	**23rd** 3:5
utility 33:8	57:17 61:21	**wild** 37:17	17:17 23:10,11	
	63:9 66:14	**willingness** 27:6	24:10 27:20,21	**3**
V	**want** 4:11 10:22	**wiser** 43:19	46:3 52:9	**309** 1:15 3:7
v 23:9	14:4 28:22	**wish** 45:6 49:5		**37** 16:12 45:22
valuable 33:16	35:20 47:8	**witness** 67:12	**Z**	**38** 45:19 46:3,7
33:21	48:14 53:21	**women** 4:12		
value 28:17 34:7	54:18 63:11	**wonder** 64:9	**0**	**4**
37:6 40:6	**wanted** 20:14	**wonderful**		**4** 46:3
41:19,20,22	27:22	25:14	**1**	
50:19 53:6	**warrants** 23:16	**word** 17:19	**1** 44:10 66:7	**5**
55:9,11 56:2	26:20 49:14	**wording** 21:22	**1:00** 1:17 3:4	**5** 66:8
varied 33:10	**Washington**	**words** 19:5	**1:45** 45:15	**5th** 7:13
various 6:2	1:14,16 3:6,8	21:22 22:5	**10** 67:17	
23:20 34:7	56:13	34:1 35:10	**11** 44:7	**6**
vast 34:10 40:17	**wasting** 42:13	65:8,20	**12** 30:17 44:10	**6** 46:3
53:3	**watch** 29:1	**work** 13:5 18:7	**16th** 3:11	
verify 6:13	**way** 14:15 20:12	18:22 29:7,22	**17** 16:13 46:6	**7**
versus 26:9 56:4	20:16 21:14	36:14 54:12		**7** 46:3
64:7	25:11 30:2	60:9	**2**	**702** 5:7,9
vetted 49:9	38:10 41:21	**workable** 53:17	**2** 44:7	
Vice 7:15	54:12 55:14	**worked** 14:5	**2:05** 66:20	**8**
view 9:10 19:8	62:3,12 67:10	**working** 4:13	**2005** 64:14	**800** 1:15 3:7
31:5 33:7 42:5	**we'll** 44:4	14:13 17:14	**20052** 1:16	**8th** 7:14
42:21 43:7	**we're** 3:6 15:16	18:19 43:4	**2006** 64:14	
62:8 65:8	20:11 24:2	56:22	**2009** 65:1	
viewed 40:17	28:4 46:18	**workload** 60:22	**2011** 65:2	
views 7:16 10:21	47:11 51:15	**world** 33:9	**2013** 67:13	
12:9 14:1	52:4 59:1 61:8	**worried** 28:21	**2014** 1:10 3:5,11	
29:11,12 36:17	61:10	**worse** 53:18	67:17	
36:20 48:15	**we've** 5:1 11:4	**worth** 56:2,6	**215** 1:5 4:3 5:7	
violation 40:16	14:5,9,10,12	**wouldn't** 22:10	6:15 7:21 9:1,5	
virtually 50:6	18:3 27:13	53:21,22 57:22	9:10 12:3,6	
voice 59:17	55:15 59:9	58:3 63:20	19:4 21:22	
voluminous	61:9 63:6,14	**written** 16:16	25:4 26:8 27:3	
61:12	66:12	46:10	27:13 31:4,17	
voluntarily 13:9	**website** 45:2	**wrong** 40:13	33:9,11,18	
vote 63:19	**week** 7:18 17:4		34:1 37:4,9	
voting 56:19	**weighed** 31:1	**X**	38:13,16 44:3	
	weight 22:6		53:7 60:1 63:3	
W	37:14	**Y**	64:16,21 65:6	
Wald 2:5 3:17	**Welcome** 3:2	**Yeah** 51:2	**21st** 1:15 3:7	

www.ingramcontent.com/pod-product-compliance
Lightning Source LLC
Chambersburg PA
CBHW080516290526
45790CB00006B/2191